Then & Now
ELY

The Red Arrows fly past. This perfectly timed shot by Brian Lane has caught the Red Arrows as they flew over Ely to mark the second official visit of Queen Elizabeth II, with the Duke of Edinburgh, in 1987, for the distribution of the Royal Maundy at the cathedral. This shows the Market Place when it was still marked out as a car park; much-used except on market days. Then, there were three traditional red phone boxes on the left and the ground was covered with tarmac, not the pinkish-red bricks of today.

Front cover: J.F. Burrows' newsagents and booksellers, established 1899. His son Percy, seen here around 1935 in the doorway, has been followed in the business by his children, grandchildren Geoffrey and Ann and great-granddaughter Annabelle.

Then & Now
ELY

COMPILED BY PAMELA BLAKEMAN

TEMPUS

Co-op Gala. Ely Co-operative Society sports on the Barrack Field on the north side of Barton Road in June 1924. The *Ely Standard* reporter said, 'It is computed… about 600 children' took part and watched the sports and amusements. Those taking part assembled in Broad Street and, led by the band, went first to the market place where the fancy dress costumes, decorated doll's prams, cycles and hoops were judged. Then they went to the sports field 'where the children were "drawn up" in mass formation ready for the attack on the good things provided for tea'.

First published 2002

Tempus Publishing Limited
The Mill, Brimscombe Port,
Stroud, Gloucestershire, GL5 2QG

British Library Cataloguing in Publication Data.
A catalogue record for this book is available from the British Library.

ISBN 0 7524 2652 4

Typesetting and origination by Tempus Publishing Limited
Printed in Great Britain by Midway Colour Print, Wiltshire

CONTENTS

A.V. Bonnett & Son. In 1835 Foster's Bank opened on the corner of High Street and Chequer Lane and later the present building was erected on the same site. From 1904 the Capital and Counties Bank occupied the building until it became Lloyds in 1918. Bonnett's began trading as a baker's in 1921 and opened a first-floor restaurant here in 1925. During the Second World War the firm supplied bread to the USAF under a War Department contract. Popular on market days, Bonnett's served good traditional meals – meat and two veg followed by apple pie and custard – until the last day of business for the bakery and restaurant on 1 November 1997. The snack bar continued for a short time. Bonnett's also had premises in Broad Street during the 1930s and into the 1950s.

ACKNOWLEDGEMENTS

I have very much appreciated the help of many people, most of them born and bred in Ely, who have helped in a variety of ways and have allowed me to make use of their photographs. There is not space to mention each one but I would particularly like to thank Frances and Tony Fletcher, Sam Lawrence, Chris Jakes and the staff at the Cambridgeshire Collection for the 'then' photographs on pages 18, 51 and 75, and the editor and staff of the *Ely Standard*, the Trustees of Ely Museum and also Cambridge Newspapers for those on pages 33 and 38. I have made every effort to obtain the necessary permission for the use of all photographs not taken by myself and am extremely grateful to photographers Steve Cole, who took the 'Now' photographs for the 'River' chapter and also those on pages 23 and 45; Brian Lane (opposite title page, and 'then' pictures on 23 and 45), Donald Monk ('then' pictures on 17, 40, 44, 49, 53, 73), Alan Mott ('then' 59), Nick Heddle ('now' 67), Kenneth Sellers ('then' 76) and for permission to use the 'then' picture on page 78, which is acknowledged as © Crown Copyright 1987/MOD.

Introduction

Where have the photographs come from? Many, both new and old, that attempt to record changes during the last forty to fifty years, are from the author's own collection, many provided by others who have also lived in Ely for most of their lives. Most of those chosen could equally fit into different sections of the book, or into more than one. Those who know the city well will realise that it would need a larger book than this to record all the recent changes, but I hope this will be a reminder of many of them.

Ten years ago – even five years ago – this would have been a very different collection of photographs; as with so many places, particularly in East Anglia, Ely is changing extremely rapidly. As archaeological evidence grows, our perception is even altering over exactly where the settlement that was to become Ely began. The city we see today is grouped around the cathedral, begun in the eleventh century, which followed St Etheldreda's seventh-century monastic foundation. This central area has, in many ways, improved during the last quarter of a century, as a number of run-down properties have been demolished and the small derelict sites have been filled with new houses. On the outskirts, new housing estates are mushrooming, so the population is growing and is now estimated at around 14,000; an increase of about 3,000 since the 1991 census. Expansion to the south is limited, partly because of environmental considerations and partly because the road and land are below sea level for perhaps a couple of miles round the perimeter and beyond; black peaty fen soil does not take kindly to development. Business is flourishing along a former green road, Angel Drove, with the success of the Cambridgeshire Business Park. On Station Road is Standen's engineering works and a large Tesco store which, with the King's School, are the city's largest employers. An overall change is particularly noticeable in the increase in road traffic and the growth of trees.

What of business in the city centre? Of course there are retail shops, and a handful of nationally-known stores have gathered around the new shopping centre – The Cloisters – which opened in 1999. A number of small retail outlets of long standing are closing, particularly in the High Street, and being replaced by others, and Ely now has two night clubs and a number of good leisure facilities. However, there is no jam factory, no leather factory, no nearby beet sugar factory, and farming employs fewer people than in the past, so a great many Ely residents commute daily to Cambridge and London by car and train. In spite of this, the two busy market days continue to attract people from nearby villages, and since the nineteenth century Ely has been fortunate to develop as a major railway junction, so an increasing number of tourists come by train. The majority come to visit the Cathedral of the Holy and Undivided Trinity, but others have found that there is more to enjoy. There is a National Stained Glass Museum within the cathedral, an Ely Museum which unfolds the interesting story of the area, a themed Tourist Information Centre, which tells of Oliver Cromwell and his time, and in addition there is the riverside which, with the nearby Jubilee Park, provides a pleasant area in which to relax.

Administration too has changed; the first meeting of the Urban District Council took place in 1895, the last early in 1974, since when Ely has had a City of Ely Council with parish status and has been part of East Cambridgeshire at district council level.

Some things endure; the city of Ely, set on a low hill rising above the surrounding black fenland, is still crowned by a magnificent medieval cathedral, a landmark for many miles as it has been for pilgrims throughout the ages. Still the pilgrims come, many to see the cathedral and to worship there, many to wonder at the former monastic buildings and to enjoy the city.

The University of Cambridge Aerial Photography Unit took this view in May 1981 when the layout near the west front of the cathedral was slightly different and the fair, held annually in May and October, was in the market place. Most of the changes can be seen in the top left-hand corner: the Rex Cinema has been demolished to make way for Boots the chemist, the post office is still next to the Club Hotel and Tesco's supermarket has not been revamped. It is misleading that vehicles are shown next to the post office yard as this was only an unofficial park. The Broad Street car park is shown at the top right. The cathedral appears to be as it is now but as over twelve million pounds has been spent on the fabric since 1986 its appearance from the air is deceptive.

Chapter 1

THE RIVER GREAT OUSE AT ELY

William Dew, supervisor at Roswell Pits, with his dog Rose, c. 1900, bringing in reeds for thatching. His great nephew said 'He was responsible for hiring the men, putting them to work, maintaining the equipment and buildings… keeping tally of the barge loads of gault (Kimmeridge clay) dispatched to various drainage boards'. He and his wife Jane lived at Roswell Pits cottage close to their work. Willows – osiers – for basket making were also grown near Ely, where there were about forty basket makers in the 1870s, and baskets were sold throughout the area, particularly at the market at Bury St Edmunds.

Cuckoo Bridge, photographed by Doug Unwin on 29 January 1939 (top), when it was struck by a barge

due to the high level of the water that winter. The bridge was replaced by two successive wooden structures, the second in 1952. This became unsafe in 2000 and a new and more permanent bridge was erected at cost of £90,000. It was officially opened on 26 January 2001 by Ian Sharpe, who had won two silver medals and one bronze when he represented England in the Power Olympics at Sydney in 2000. The public footpath, for many years used by workers taking a short cut to the beet sugar factory as well as by families on Sunday afternoon walks, was once again useable.

The view looking across Roswell Pits, *c.* 1970 (bottom) from which Kimmeridge clay (locally known as gault) was extracted to build up the river banks to prevent the surrounding low-lying – below sea level – land from being flooded. This outcrop of clay has yielded many fossils of marine dinosaurs. The view has changed little but the pits remain deep and dangerous so walkers, who follow the Ely nature trail along the narrow path, are warned to take care. This trail was prepared in 1970 but has since been extended and includes Springhead Lane, known over the years as Love Lane, Kiln Lane and Blythinghale Lane.

Once the home of the Merry family in around 1920, who were noted for catching eels which at one time were plentiful in the river at Ely. This small cottage (top) was situated on the far side of the river in the area known as Babylon, somewhere close to the 1964 Lincoln Bridge. One of the family, James, was presented in 1906, with a testimonial written on vellum by The Royal Humane Society in recognition of his rescue of twenty people from the river. Fellow citizens presented him with a chiffonier, dining table and a purse of gold in appreciation of his bravery. The site is now occupied by Lovey's Marine-Ely Marina, which has moorings for 200 boats.

A group of local children pose on the quayside in 1937 (bottom) when the river level was higher than normal; today the river does not flood every spring. In the back row, from left to right are Doreen Webb, Mary Lee, Joan Lee, Lily Webb, Ivy Salmons holding Bill Salmons, and Sid Salmons. In the front row are Lilian Salmons, Pam Bidwell, Arthur Bidwell and Doreen Salmons. Behind to the right and today almost hidden by the bushes is the stone building, once Marche's brewery which, after a variety of uses, now houses East Cambridgeshire District Council offices on the first floor and the Babylon Gallery run by Arts Development in East Cambridgeshire (Adec). The latter houses interesting and prestigious exhibitions of paintings, pottery and other crafts. On the left is the building which now houses Waterside Antiques.

THE FLOODS, ELY.
MAR. 18, 1937. 20 FT

Waterside, once the main route into the city, with the Quay in the foreground around 1912 (top). The second house from the left was the Queen's Head. Set back in the early photograph was the home of the brewing family of Harlock; the brewery chimney behind has gone and the house is covered with creeper. The next building on the corner of Back Lane was for many years the Haven, a Diocesan home for unmarried women; until the end of July it was the Waterside Tea Rooms. This and the distant view of Crown Point are now hidden by a large willow tree and the quay is hidden by pleasure boats.

The former Ship Inn, which dates back at least as far the seventeenth century, in its post-Second World War mock Tudor disguise, is partly hidden by the willow tree (bottom). This view was taken before the construction of the Riverside Walk, which opened in the late 1960s, and had necessitated the removal of both Steward's Maltings (next to the Cutter) and the Ship Inn. Today, large willow trees obstruct the view even more but part of the Ely Maltings, previously behind the Ship, is seen on the right. On the opposite side of the river the boathouses of Cambridge University and King's

School Ely remain though most of Babylon is now a large marina.

A Shell Mex and BP barge, in the early 1930s (top), waits ready to deliver oil to the pumping stations which were essential to the drainage of the Fens. Pumping stations where engines were driven by steam, then diesel oil until electricity took over, replaced hundreds of windmills that had been dotted all over the Fens. Behind them, in front of the old granary, stand a car and five large vehicles, one horse-drawn, which brought the oil to the barges. On the left stands Mr Smith, next to him Ernest Mann and then Jack Reeve. The town houses, just glimpsed to the right of the house on the left, were built in 1971 but again trees hide part of the view.

The Boat House, seen below in around 1955, probably dates back around 300 years. In the 1950s Mr. Appleyard, last in a line of seven generations of boat builders, sold his business to Harry Lincoln. It then became known as Lincoln's Boatyard, until his retirement. In 1985 the Old Boathouse Restaurant opened which, particularly in summer months, adds to the attractions of the riverside. Edwin (Ted) Appleyard lived in the house furthest to the left. He loved to cruise on the Fen waterways, particularly in his pleasure boat Shellfen II which he bought in 1985. Latterly he enjoyed a

ride around Ely on his Sinclair C5 battery powered tricycle; he died in June 1995 at over ninety years of age.

The top picture was taken before the centre of the view was filled by houses in 1892, when the Cutter Inn sold ale brewed at Cutlack's Littleport brewery. Babylon, where the large tree is, then had perhaps a dozen or more houses on it; the railway line cut through the gardens further to the left. All trains going to and from Ely still run on this stretch of line; they connect directly with Peterborough, King's Lynn, Norwich, Ipswich, Stansted, London and further afield to Liverpool, Cardiff and other destinations. The recent view not only puts emphasis on the number of boats in the area but also shows how the type of boat has changed. New houses have been built to the right of the Cutter.

This rare view of the towpath (bottom), taken from Ely High Bridge, dates from before 1896 when the railway bridge, made partly of wood, was replaced by a stronger one of wrought iron. This was once a busy waterway with barges and Fen lighters, transporting coal, grain and farm produce often to or from the port of King's Lynn where Ely ale was sold as long ago as the thirteenth century. For many years this part of the towpath has provided a place for interesting country walks looking at the boats, the ducks and swans. During the last forty years the river has become increasingly busy with pleasure boats; many are moored along this part of the river as it flows through Ely. On the left of the path is the Bridge Fen Marina run by the Wenn family and, of course, the cathedral is still there but well-hidden.

193. ELY FROM ROAD BRIDGE

"COOPER'S ARMS" FISHING CLUB. ELY. SEP. 1922.

Fishing in 1922 (top). In the past, four Ely pubs, the Marquis of Granby in Victoria Street, the Highflyer in Newnham Street, the Cutter near the river and the Cooper's Arms in Waterside all had thriving fishing clubs. Today the Cutter and the Highflyer pubs flourish but the Cooper's Arms is the only fishing club to remain. This club began sometime in the nineteenth century and its members still catch bream, roach, perch, tench, pike, zander and eels in the Ouse, near the Cresswells. The treasurer, John Smith, is not in the lower photograph, taken by secretary John Dickens in 2002, but the chairman Roger Spencer is on the extreme right. The two fishermen who look as though they haven't decided whether to stand or sit are Darren Parsons and Richard (Chalkie) White.

A children's fancy dress competition, to mark the Coronation of Elizabeth II in 1953, held down Waterside almost opposite to the Waterside Antiques Centre, then a disused granary, where tea was provided after the judging. Many local people can be seen, from Mrs Parker on the left, Mrs Cornwell, Mrs Mynott, Vernon Cross, Percy Cole, Mrs Haylock, Mrs Ladds and Mrs Ireland. At the far end is Ann Barton wearing a halo-like bonnet made of paper, as were all the costumes,

probably because during the Second World War new clothes could only be bought in exchange for coupons. All wartime rationing ended in July 1954.

CHURCH CONGRESS, ELY, 1910 PASSING DOWN HIGH STREET

The Church Congress in 1910 (top), after tea at the Corn Exchange, progresses along High Street toward the Lamb corner. The cathedral choir is in the foreground followed by other diocesan choirs. The procession passes shop fronts still in place today; from the left Legge's (now Gibb's), Pledger's which closed in the mid-1950s (now Argos, after a time as Lipton's and then Presto) and Cutlack's (the single storey section was sold and rebuilt in 1986 providing a shop for frequently changing shoe retailers). On the other side of Chequer Lane was a bank for many years which after much recent refurbishment opened as a Clintons card shop. A little further along is Lloyd's chemist, for a time Savory and Moore's, where from at least the sixteenth century was the Bell Hotel which closed in 1959; in the distance is the small building, now Tea for Two. Today's view shows the street closed to traffic on a Saturday morning; since autumn 2000 it has been shut off between 10.00a.m. and 4.00p.m. The one car in the street obviously entered before 10.00am!

The cathedral west front floodlit by Calor gas, *c.* 1960 (top): an advertising venture by Cutlack's ironmongers (established 1841 and the oldest business in the city). The railings and hedge have gone but the cannon from Russia remains. Ely's west front has been asymmetric since the fall of the north-west transept, perhaps in the seventeenth century or earlier; exactly when and why it fell is not certain. On the right is the richly decorated front of the south-west transept. The lower part of the tower and the transept were built in the late-twelfth century, the top section with the turrets added at the beginning of the fifteenth. In front is the thirteenth-century entrance known as the Galilee Porch. Today, in daylight the view is equally impressive; the fourteenth-century Lady Chapel is on the left and during the evening Ely's unique fourteenth-century central octagon and lantern tower, hidden here behind the west tower, is floodlit.

The Lady Chapel in the 1950s (top) when the chapel was once again, after over 500 years as a parish church, in the care of the Dean and Chapter. Little idea of its size – the largest chapel dedicated to Mary, the Mother of Christ, in the country – or of the richness of the carvings can be appreciated in small photographs. The scene in July 2002 when the floor, except for a central line of memorials, had been removed so that an under floor heating system could be installed and a new floor of Purbeck marble put in place. The latter is to have sixteen panels each patterned with one of five designs. But first, the archaeologists searched; they found fragments of skeletons and a stone sarcophagus that may have been that of John of Wisbech, the monk in charge of building the Lady Chapel during the first half of the fourteenth century. Today, silhouetted against the east window is the controversial stone statue of Mary; her dress is blue and her hair gold. This and the bronze in the south transept of the cathedral, of Mary meeting Christ after the resurrection, are by David Wynne. The chapel is to be re-dedicated on 7 September 2002 when the heating system, new cushions and the Purbeck marble floor, will be complete.

The entrance to the Processional Way between the wars (top) when the door led outside to a slightly untidy area between the north choir aisle and the Lady Chapel; here was the building which housed the organ blower and a store for the cathedral flower arrangers. In December 2000 a new Processional Way, built on the site of a medieval passage, was completed. It was dedicated by the Right Reverend Dr Anthony Russell, Bishop of Ely on St Etheldreda's Day, 23 June 2001. Here there are windows designed by Helen Whittaker and made at the Keith Barley studio in York and oak roof timbers decorated with wooden bosses carved by Peter Ball, whose work is also seen above the cathedral pulpit. On the floor is a beautifully cut stone panel carved by Cardozo Kindersley, which reads: 'This Processional Way stands on the foundation of the Lady Chapel Passage used by the pilgrims to Ely. Beneath the floor lie the mortal remains of twenty-seven persons from the wider monastic community re-interred during building work AD 2000.' Hidden away on the inner side of the passage are welcome cloakrooms.

1566, when it was moved from the lean-to church on the north side of the cathedral into the Lady Chapel the parish name changed to Holy Trinity. In 1938 this parish was joined with St Mary's to form the Parish of Ely. The graveyard continued to be used until the 1850s; most of the remaining memorial stones were cleared in the 1960s. Today it is used as a place for relaxation and occasionally the venue for fêtes, fairs etc. On 3 June 2002 celebrations to mark the 50th Jubilee of Queen Elizabeth II took place here and on the Palace Green opposite, as well as in other parts of the city.

Cross Green, *c.* 1930 (top) when it was the churchyard for Ely's second parish of Holy Cross. From

Ely Cathedral Choir in 1920 (bottom). Back row, from left to right: Eddie Scott, Robert Pettit, Cyril Northrop. Second row: Charles Bush, Joe Woods, Frank Holmes, Charles Millis, Robert (Bob) Morris, Philip Andrews, Eric Aveling, E. Tingay, Kenneth Cornwell. Third row: Sidney Martin, Noel Ponsonby (organist), the Revd J.H. Crosby, H. Boulter (headmaster), George Jones. Front row: Herbert Chinery, Leonard Bush, John Clements, Percy Tharby, Lancelot Beamiss, Cecil Eames and Gerald Kemp. In contrast, an informal picture of the choir after the marriage of Margaret Bullock and Derek Tighe on 30 June 1990. The Precentor, the Revd Michael Tavinor, is on the left, with lay clerks Peter Heald, Harold Lindsay, Peter North, Alan Lodder and, eighth from the right at the front, soloist choirboy George Bartle.

The Bishop's Palace. The façade is little changed since Bishop Alcock's fifteenth-century east tower was linked in the seventeenth century to Bishop Goodrich's sixteenth-century long gallery. The Bishop of Ely has not lived in the palace since the beginning of the Second World War; during the war the Red Cross and St John Ambulance organisations ran a convalescent home for servicemen there. From 1946 to 1983 the Palace school for handicapped children occupied the building and since 1986 it has been a Sue Ryder Care home known as the Old Palace. Here, over forty physically handicapped men and women of all ages, many unable to walk, receive the special care that they need day and night. On 13 July, during Ely Folk weekend, colourful Morris, Molly, Country and other groups danced their way round the city centre. Here they are seen on the area in front of the cathedral which was paved in 1995.

Peace Day in the High Street (bottom). This is one of a series of images taken by Tom Bolton in May 1919. The shops, with all windows shuttered, are difficult to identify; probably, from the right, Home and Colonial Stores, G. and J. Peck Ltd, Charles Estlin, draper (with the Pullars of Perth sign), W. Lincolne, chemists, F. Butteriss, men's outfitters and, on the corner with High Street passage, Hayward & Son, furnishers and clothiers. All these shops have changed; Barries, formerly the Home and Colonial, closed at the end of June and next door a Pizza Express is newly opened. There are also two building societies, a sports shop and a dress shop.

The Good Friday ecumenical procession is on its way to the market place where a short open air service was held.

On the market place in October 1990 (top), Mayor Brian Ashton declares Ely Fair open after reading the charter. In 1992 the fair was moved from this site, traditional from medieval times, to Broad Street car park (opened in the 1960s) where, unusually, it was opened by the newly-appointed Town Crier, Averil Hayter. She was accompanied by Mayor Shirley Overall's consort and husband, Terry, who rang the hand bell to mark the beginning of the ceremony. Ely Fair – once known as St Etheldreda's and by the alternative name of St Audrey's – is held twice yearly in May and October, dates which mark the feast of St Etheldreda and the date of her first translation.

A celebration to mark the Coronation of Edward VII in 1902 (bottom). On the left, the side of the Corn Exchange, from the right part of the Club Hotel, Bolton and Churchyard (once the Post Office) City Temperance Hotel, the home of the two Miss Muriels, the White Hart Hotel and A.B. Laxon, grocer, described as the 'cheapest house in Ely'. Part of Ely's Jubilee celebrations on 3 June was a classic car show. The Club Hotel building is still here on the right but new shops and the entrance to the Cloisters shopping area, opened in November 1999, replace others. The Miss Muriels' home is now

a fish and chip shop and café and the White Hart building has shops on the ground floor.

The Thursday Market, *c.* 1963 (top) with a van advertising Fyffes bananas is close to the 1847 Corn Exchange, which was replaced by shops in the 1960s. In the middle distance, on the west side of the Market Place (renamed Dolphin Lane), is A.A. Bowgen, Forum Ltd., Elizabeth of Ely and on the corner Kempton's greengrocers. Look at the changed rooftops above the Sandwich Bar, now on the corner site, and the building to its left. Market Street is glimpsed to the right beyond the distinctive 'Ely Ales The Club Hotel' sign and today beyond the clock. From the days of the monastery there has been a market here though until 1801 it was held on a Saturday. Today there is a traditional market on Thursdays and a craft, collectors and curiosities market on Saturdays, with a Farmer's Market on the second and fourth Saturdays in the month.

Aquafest has been organized by the Rotary Club of Ely and held on – and in – the River Great Ouse near the Grassyards and the Babylon Gallery (formerly Marche's brewery) since 1978. That year the requisite raft race from Ely High Bridge to Willow Walk was won by the British Sugar Corporation's 'A' team (bottom). Again on 7 July in 2002, the twenty-fifth anniversary raft race took place, not as originally, but from just beyond the Babylon Gallery to the Cutter Inn. This was for the second year running won by The Hole in the Wall with an amazing time of eighteen minutes and twenty seconds. In second place came Ely Tennis Club Veterans who were soon followed by the *Ely Weekly News* team.

Babylon in 1973 (top), before the area became Ely Marina, with a funfair, steam engine and many people taking part in the memorable thirteenth centenary celebrations to mark the foundation of the monastery by St Etheldreda in 673. It was a wonderful year in Ely with a variety of events ranging from street fairs, an inland waterways boat rally, exhibitions, concerts and special services. Ely won television competition 'Its a Knockout' which added to the fun but, more importantly, the year ended with the Queen's visit. This was followed the next year by royal confirmation of Ely's title of 'City' and the appointment of the first mayor. The marina now has moorings for 200 boats and extends between river and railway line.

The newly-formed Great Eastern Railway band formed near Ely station probably on Peace Day 1919. Various buildings connected with the railway goods yard, seen in the photograph below were demolished many years ago. Then a motorail on which cars could travel to Scotland and one or two small factories were built on this site. (The advertisements are for local businesses; Freeman, Hardy and Willis, shoe retailer originally on Fore Hill, and M.A. Briggs, ladies fashions in Broad Street where Ely Upholstery and Carpet Services are today). In 1994 Tesco, one of Ely's largest employers, opened here and provided a large car park for customers. The view taken

from the same place today shows only a row of parked cars in front of a hedge but at a slightly different angle part of Tesco's store is visible.

35

ENGLAND'S TWO QUEENS
AT ELY CATHEDRAL. 21 JAN 1938

Top: Queen Mary as she was at 11.45a.m. on Friday 21 January 1938, about to enter the west door on an unofficial visit to Ely Cathedral with her daughter-in-law who later became Queen Elizabeth, the Queen Mother. Many other members of the present royal family have made official visits to Ely, from the Queen to Princess Margaret, Princess Diana, the Duchess of Kent and, as chairman of the appeal for Ely Cathedral, The Duke of Edinburgh on a number of occasions. In 1988 on 27 June, after her second unofficial visit, the Queen Mother, dressed in pink, leaves the cathedral accompanied by The Dean, the Very Revd William (Bill) Patterson.

Sheep graze on a field to the south of the cathedral (bottom), apparently on the field that is now a car and coach park opposite one of the King's School's sports fields where cricket is often played during the summer months. A gable of the Black Hostelry, in Firmary Lane, is on the right, below the end of the cathedral's south transept just above the trees. The wall can be seen in both photographs but trees obscure part of the previous view. Both photographs give a clear view of the west tower and the octagon and lantern; the latter built of wood and covered with lead. Known as the Ship of the Fens the

cathedral can be seen for many miles across the countryside on a clear day or floodlit at night.

Queen Elizabeth plants a tree near the river on 23 November 1973 (top); she is watched by Urban District Council chairman, Councillor Stanley Cornwell. HRH the Duke of Edinburgh also planted a tree, a maple, near the river, in the Jubilee Gardens on 11 February 2002 to mark the official opening. A stone commemorates this, bearing the inscription: 'EIIR Jubilee gardens opened by HRH the Duke of Edinburgh KGKT to celebrate the Golden Jubilee Year of Queen Elizabeth 11th February 2002'. He was assisted by Rebecca Morley and watched by Councillor Valerie Leake and children from St Mary's Church of England School.

An aerial view probably taken in the
1960s in which many earlier
features can be seen. On the left were
part of the goods yard, a gasometer and
the small 1930s swimming pool. On the
corner of Broad Street is the Rifleman
public house, sometime the Volunteer,
with the Royal Oak opposite. Along
Station Road is King Charles in the Oak
and The Angel, the latter, since 1997,
Angel House, offices for international
research consultants. The view from
Annesdale to beyond the coal
merchant's brick house which faces
onto Station Road is dominated by the
Hereward Works of Standen

Chapter 3
WORK

Engineering Ltd. Close to the railway
siding, left of the railway bridge, is the
dock; here coal, brought by train, was
loaded onto barges to be taken to the
pumping stations. To the extreme right
is the 1896 railway bridge which crosses
the Ouse.

Standen's, referred to above, was founded in St Ives and in 1936 opened an Ely branch in premises in Lynn Road. After the Second World War, the business, which made agricultural machinery, expanded and in 1959 re-located to Station Road. The Lynn Road premises which had, at times, offices and flats above, became Danske furniture showroom which closed around 1990. In 2001 the derelict building was replaced by The Paddock, a group of houses. This type of small improvement has occurred in other parts of the city, for example on Cambridge Road both the bus station and a garage have been replaced by houses.

Ely Service Motor Company in 1951 (bottom) with Mr Yardy's 1948 Hillman Minx de Luxe AEB 593; over the years it was mostly Austin and Hillman cars that were sold here. The business was started in 1930 by local entrepreneur Russell Wright, best remembered as a butcher in the High Street, who after a year sold to Charles Hull. Mr Hull and his son Tony ran the firm here until 1994 when the business was re-formed and moved to Lancaster Way Business Park. The Lynn Road premises, now known as the Lighthouse Centre, house a bookshop and Ely

Christian Fellowship. The next building, once the office of the Urban District Council, is now an accountants.

H ire cars await their instructions,
c. 1920 (top). From the left is an
Iris Landaulette, Ford T, 15 hp Wolseley

and a visiting Siddeley-Deasy. Alexander
Cass began his business opposite The
Cathedral Centre (Ely Library from the
1960s until 2000) but moved during the
First World War to these larger premises.
He sold the business in 1940 and it
became Nice's and later Birch's. The
ground floor of the building facing on
to St Mary's Street has now been
returned to the use and appearance of
pre-garage days when there were private
houses there. The conversion received a
Civic Trust Award. The remainder of
the garage premises is now a small car
park. In today's photograph part of the
Lamb Hotel is to the right.

In 1958 the gas works and showroom closed after gas manufacture stopped in Ely and a supply was piped from Cambridge. After Ely was converted to receive natural gas from the North Sea in 1969 the site, with that on the corner of Station Road and Potters Lane where the former Black Swan public house had been, was cleared. In the early 1960s Graven & Son, a longstanding Ely firm, opened a car showroom and filling station which was later taken over by Trigon. The garage closed and in 1995 houses were built; it is typical of Ely in the twenty-first century that

this sort of area, as well as a number of small city centre derelict sites, is now occupied by houses.

J.M. Harvey had large premises here from the end of the nineteenth century until the 1950s; the firm occupied the area from No. 23, later

Theobald's, to the corner of High Street Passage and sold, from the left, curtain materials, ladies and childrens underwear, millinery, ladies and gentlemens fashions. Since then smaller shops have changed more than once; Jaremcio's, once Ablett's shoe shop, is now a shoe repairers; Theobalds closed in 1982; Boots has moved to Market Street and been succeeded in turn by United News, and in June 2002 by a Spar store. On the corner with High Street Passage the Mayfair has given way to Oxfam. In spite of all the changes at ground level the earlier façades above the shops remain in this part of the High Street.

Mr Sidney Theobald stands proudly in his draper's shop in High Street, *c.* 1969 (bottom), which he opened in March 1958 and closed twenty-four years later. Mr Theobald served Ely well as a councillor, and as Mayor during 1975-76. These premises are now a travel agents and a Sue Ryder charity shop but another shop, the City Cycle Centre in Market Street, has developed a haberdashery and needlecraft department through the toy department on the ground floor. Bridget stands here ready to sell sale goods as was Mr Theobald over thirty years ago. This building became the main post office towards the end of the nineteenth century; it was rebuilt in 1891 and the

position of the initials VR can still be seen near the entrance and a stone crown is still above the door.

Peck's – G. & J. Peck Ltd, ironmongers, opened on the Market Place, where Cheffins is now, in 1846 but soon moved to premises which go back to the seventeenth century in the High Street – premises that went through to Market Street. Everything was sold from an ounce of nails to galvanised zinc baths, from Wellington boots to kitchen utensils. In 1998 the firm closed in High Street but continued in Lisle Lane where they had opened in 1978. There the emphasis is on the sale and repair of farm machinery and garden equipment; combines to lawn mowers. Part of the High Street shop front was totally changed in the 1920s when the bay window was removed and replaced with a large plate-glass window. Now the front has been changed again and above ground-floor level small framed windows abound! This upper part of the building has been converted into flats and a Pizza Express opened in the High Street in July 2000. The area between the two streets was demolished and a small block of flats built. In Market Street, W.H. Smith has opened but the next door shop remains empty.

The Quay Brewery in the 1920s (top) with a row of 'Cutlack and Harlock Ltd Ely' Thorney lorries waiting to be loaded. By the middle of the nineteenth century this was one of four main breweries in Ely. Eventually, after amalgamation had led to the transfer of brewing to the Fore Hill premises, mineral water was produced here for some years. The cellar of the building on the left was the brewery barrel store now about to be converted into three residences, surrounded as it is by new houses built in 2001-02 and a building site. Broad Street and the cathedral are in the background. Part of the cellars along Hythe Lane were used as a public air-raid shelter at the beginning of the Second World War; the spine-chilling wail of the air-raid warning sounded in Ely on Sunday 3 September 1939 but the all clear was soon heard. (Perhaps this was a trial to make sure it worked?) The warning was not heard here again for some nine months. That same year another part of this Quay Brewery was the scene of a spectacular fire – though not due to the war – on the evening of Wednesday 27 September when thousands of bags, stored for the Beet Sugar Factory, ignited. All of Ely rushed to watch the fire and the fire brigade, under the command of local solicitor, Colonel Archer.

The Thursday market, in front of the 1847 Corn Exchange (top). The latter was in use both as a corn exchange and as a public hall until shortly before its demolition in the 1960s. It was replaced, as has already been shown, by shops. The white horizontal line which marks the position of a canopy until its removal, *c*. 2000 still dominates this building. The only point of reference is the side view of the small gable which is part of the building where a travel agent's is now; it is on the east side of the market place, in the photos immediately to the left of both the Corn Exchange and the 1960s shops.

The Cattle Market (bottom), which opened in November 1846, occupied a site off Newnham Street. Auctioneer George Comins appears to have been selling pigs as the rear view of one can be seen on the left. Cattle and sheep were also auctioned but no animals have been sold here since September 1981. After that cars, and then all types of second-hand goods and farm produce, including chickens, were auctioned on Thursdays until shortly before a new shopping development began with the opening of Waitrose in March 1992. The site of the old cattle market is now part-

delivery area, part-car park which serve the Cloisters.

Known locally as the 'jam' factory, probably because since it opened the factory has changed owners a number of times, or perhaps because of the smell both of the jam and of the barrels of pulp stored at the back. It opened on this site as Grangers Fruit Preserving Company in 1890 and within twenty years the premises were rebuilt. Later it was St Martins (Eastern Ltd), makers of 'Chunky' marmalade, followed by Ticklers of Grimsby before it became Dorman Sprayers and then the Eastern Printing works. It was demolished in the 1980s and a group of houses and flats known as St Martin's Walk was built. The architecture attempts to echo the factory building.

Looking up Fore Hill, *c.* 1908 (bottom). On the right is Churchyard the ironmongers, with the Conservative Club above, then Blake's, furnishers and Woodroffe, painter. Further up, where the veterinary practice is today was G.H. King, butcher followed by Mrs Scott, basket maker, Nightingale's Eating House, Walker & Co. stores, Kempton the carpenter, International Stores, Eastman & Co., butchers and Sturton and Howard, chemists. Below the vets, Blake's had a larger shop which until this year was Courts, another furnishers; this has closed and is boarded up. Above ground floor level much remains unchanged except for Nightingale's (part of the Baron of Beef) which was replaced by J.M. Evans shop in 1959. This was

after a move from Broad Street where it had opened in the 1930s. Evans closed in October 1999 and in 2001 Griffin's Antiques opened.

FORE HILL, ELY.

The leather factory, with an adjoining shop on Fore Hill almost opposite the Conservative Club, was owned by Blakemans from the early nineteenth century until 1944. In 1973 the factory, part of which dated from 1836, and the adjoining house with the premises of Tom Bolton, photographer, and Lemmon's, family butchers, were demolished. Today most of the site is taken up by an office block and a car park for the office. The white building to the left was Marjorie's, a small self-service store, now a hairdressers. To the right of this is a small passageway where Gotobed's greengrocery shop was situated for forty or more years. Up the hill was the London Central Meat Company and then the Rose and Crown, now Gallery Frames.

Platform One, Ely railway station. Below, a new high-speed Central Railway's diesel train, class 170, is on the centre line. This line was used by through trains travelling north or south before the electrification of the London to King's Lynn line was completed in 1992. The centre line was then removed and, from the same position, the remaining two lines are hidden in today's photograph because both this platform and platform two, on the right, were widened, as was the canopy on two. The old signal box and semaphore signals have been removed and replaced by coloured light signalling. The level crossing is now automated. On platform one is a recently extended park and ride cycle rack which is increasingly popular with commuters.

Mr Overall worked at Highflyer Farm in High Barns in the early 1930s, here harvesting rye (top). Highflyer was the name of a horse that was buried nearby and of an Ely pub. Another horse called Maringo, who had once belonged to Napoleon, spent its last days at Highflyer Hall; its skeleton with one hoof set in silver is believed to be in a national museum. Around this story a confusing legend has grown up about a monument in the form of an obelisk on the Lynn Road, but there is no connection. Today a combine harvester cuts, threshes and separates in one operation, collecting the rape seed in a tank whilst chopping the rest of the plant and spreading it on the ground behind. In the distance are typical Fen horizons, low and straight, allowing the sky and wonderful sunsets to be enjoyed to the full.

Within the Parish of Ely, almost four miles to the north-east of the city, is the village of Prickwillow; here the land is flat and the soil rich and black. The house remains at the corner of Kingdon Avenue but at harvest there are no longer haystacks on the right and the group of people walking away from the village towards Ely would be very differently dressed. At the other end of the village, near the river Lark – a tributary of the Ouse – lies the Prickwillow Drainage Museum, opened in 1983, where a Mirrlees diesel pump once used for drainage can be seen. Most of the houses are traditional but there are one or two exciting late twentieth-century houses here.

Ely Road, Prickwillow, Ely.

Prickwillow Vicarage.

The Vicar, the Revd Claude Drewitt Kingdon, stands outside his home in winter (top) at a time when the Vicarage had only one or two steps to the front door. Today, due to the shrinkage of the peat soil as the drainage of the Fens continues there are two steps up from the lawn and nine steps up to the front door, and work has been done to stabilise the house. It is no longer the Vicarage although St Peter's church, consecrated in 1866, continues in use; services are usually taken by clergy from St Mary's church in Ely. The house in July 2002 is on the market at a suggested price of £450,000.

Nearer to Ely is the small hamlet of Queen Adelaide seen below in the early twentieth century; it was named, we are told, after a pub situated there. The river bridge was rebuilt in 1930 on a slightly different angle from the earlier one. There is also a railway bridge, over the loop, known as Ely South Curve, and three level crossings at each of the lines from Ely to Peterborough, King's Lynn, and Norwich. The curve 'which branches from the March line enables traffic off this route to run through Ely North Junction to Norwich or King's Lynn without troubling Ely station' (from 'Branch Lines Around March' by Vic Mitchell, Keith Smith, Christopher Awdry and Alan Mott). Today there are three business premises; a garage, a packaging firm and the Potter Group. St Etheldreda's church, built in 1883 and just seen on the left, was sold in 1978 and converted into a house.

Queen Adelaide Bridge, Ely.

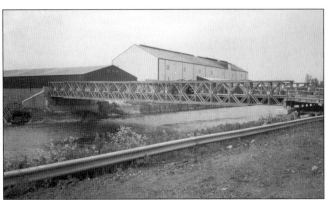

Seen from Queen Adelaide Way, the Beet Sugar Factory at Queen Adelaide opened in October 1925 and closed after the 1980-81 'campaign'. With it, in the Broad Street area of Ely, went the characteristic smell, as had that of brewing some years earlier. The Potter Group took over the former factory and the surrounding area and today its seventy acre site and 22,000 square metres of warehousing have a private rail freight terminal and a fleet of road vehicles for countrywide delivery. To facilitate this the company built a new river bridge in 1993. Examples of the goods dealt with include cars, aggregates, paper and textiles.

Three miles to the north of Ely is another hamlet, Chettisham, which had a 'permanent' railway station until 1960 when its passenger service ceased. During the electrification work at Ely during 1991-92, Ely station was closed for a time so a temporary station was built on the old site at Chettisham. Bus services were provided to link with trains. The Ely end of the platform is on the left in the early image and a train heads for Ely; in the distance is Chettisham grain store. The signal box was abolished in 1992 and has been replaced by a Permanent Electrical

Room (PER); a Peterborough train approaches from Ely.

Stuntney Old Hall was once the home of Oliver Cromwell's mother and of his uncle, Sir Thomas Steward, from whom Oliver inherited a house, property and a job in 1636. In both photographs the house looks almost the same, even if the buildings nearby have changed, but after the earlier one was taken the house fell into an even more ruinous state and in the second one is in process of being almost entirely rebuilt. The road too looks similar but the Stuntney by-pass that was completed in December 1986 employed new technology and is expected to last longer than earlier roads; it is a much faster road than the old one. The view of Ely Cathedral from this small hill is one of the best of this amazing medieval church.

A ladies fishing group taken near Ely High Bridge on 9 July 1929. Prize-winning local fisherman Harry Meadows is seated in the centre with his son Arthur on his left. Both men and women were keen anglers and often went by boat, usually the Pattie, to take part in matches. Fishermen, mainly from Sheffield were frequent visitors; they often stayed at The Kimberley in Broad Street before it was demolished to make way for NFU House in 1980 (now accountants' offices). Although not many eels are caught in the Ouse

Chapter 5

LEISURE

today more would have been found in the early part of the last century, but in the days of the monastery they had been caught in their thousands.

LADIES FISHING MATCH. ELY. JULY. 9. 1929.

On Paradise, Keith Dolby carries the Union Jack at the head of a parade of cyclists (top), all of whom had entered for cycling races in the 1955 Sports. On the left is Carol Clarke and on the right Poppy Chilvers, all three members of the Littleport Wheelers. This was the year when world cycle champion Reg Harris visited Ely. Behind is the pavilion which caught fire in May 1965 and stopped play between Ely and East Dereham cricketers. Somewhere near to the Leisure Centre and Skate Park is the site of this former pavilion; in the block on the right there are two swimming pools, one described as a training pool, twenty-five metres in length, and the other a leisure pool more suitable for children.

Ely City FC, 1949-50 (bottom). In the back row, from left to right are: Adam, J.S. Harvey, D.J. Unwin (chairman), C. Yearn, E. Barraclough, . Woodgett, G. Lawrence, K. Pope, V. Cross, E. Deards, R. Taylor, R. Brown and W. Lawrence. Middle ow: C. Latham, R. Morriss, R. Sindall, '. Joyce, D. McCusker (captain), Lockwood, S.C. Lawrence (secretary) nd D. Cranwell: Front row D. Bevan, D. Moore and F. Wilson. The Robins n 2002 with, among others, manager Kevin Pritchard at the right of the back ow and assistant manager Brett

Matthews at the other end; trainer Vince Scarrow next to him. They won the Cambridgeshire Invitation Cup Final in 2002, after thirty years.

The Committee of Ely Horticultural Society in 1938 (top) when Lionel Blackburne, fourth from the right, was Dean of Ely and to his left, B.B. Saunders, treasurer. In the centre at the front is the President, Alderman S.E. Covill with Canon T.J. Kirkland next to him and at the back the Revd G. Crisp. At the right in the middle row is secretary, Harold Trett and next to him H.A. Roythorne (seen in many photos of Ely events). The 80th anniversary photo taken in 1997 shows many well-known local people with, seated, Bernie Parker (vice-chairman), Tom Mott (trading secretary), Betty Seymour (general secretary), John Grant, Philip Peacock (chairman), George Cross, Joanne Pooley, Albert Wesley (show secretary), Joan Wesley and Gerry Rolfe (treasurer).

These productive allotments (bottom) at Barton Fields, said to be the best in Ely, were rented from the King's School by the City of Ely Council and managed by the Allotments Association. In 1997 the school required the land for its own use as part of its sports area so the allotment holders reluctantly left this pleasant, quiet site with its distant view across the Fens. It is now part of a large grassy sports field. However, there are still flourishing allotments in Bridge Fen, near Needham's play area on Back Hill, New Barns Avenue, Upherds Lane and the Thomas Parson's Charity in Deacons Lane.

class held, not at Bedford House, but at Ely Service Motor Company's premises around 1960. Many popular evening classes were held at Bedford House but reduced in number when they were transferred to the City of Ely College in Downham Road after 1972. This was when three local schools were joined to form a comprehensive school. Annette Norman, facing the camera, guides a group of Pilates enthusiasts at the City of Ely Community College. The class work to further their physical development following a method developed by Joseph Pilates.

Tutor Tom Norman talks to Reg Lupson (top), seen here with students at a motor engineering evening

Local photographer Tom Bolton used flashlight in December 1921 to take this presentation by the Wesley Guild in Ely Wesley Schoolroom (then to the rear of the present Methodist chapel) in aid of missionary funds (bottom). About a Tamil family 'who were greatly distressed about their baby… stricken with fever', it starred Freda Sykes as the baby's grandmother. From left to right are: Miss M. Lemmon, Miss L. Gibbons, Miss G. Ablett, S. Sykes, Miss L. Hall, Miss N. Tawn, B. Fenn, Miss O. Lane, Miss F. Sykes and, seated, H. Porter and E. Morgan. The City of Ely ADS production of *Lady Windermere's Fan* in 2000, with, on the left Tony Ransome who stands next to Betty Staines.

Leading lady Jill Enifer poses for the camera and on the right Mary Byfield is seated; standing near her is Ann Dix with Ed Cearns to the right.

"The Doctor & The Devil Priest."
GUILD MEMBERS. WESLEYAN. ELY. DEC.13. 1921

Chat, *c.* 1955 (top). Pausing to look at the camera are, on the left, ex-policeman Sergeant Henry Moll, with, on the right, Harry S. Speller; they are seated on the north side of the market place near the 1922 war shrine set into the wall of the Almonry garden. In 2002 people still sit and chat, especially on Market Day, but here, on a May morning, they are seated around a tree on the north-east corner of the square which was remodelled in 1993. In the background are Cheffins, Grain and Comins estate agents and the *Weekly News* office.

The Granger family (bottom), probably taking afternoon tea, in the garden of Vineyard House in May 1896. After the Grangers left the house in the 1930s it was occupied by the Pritchards, Arnolds and Summersons and was linked with the Fore Hill brewery for many years. In the year 2002 three generations of an Ely family have a less formal meal outside the same summer house accompanied by Max, a Jack Russell terrier and Lucy, a King Charles spaniel. Typically trees have grown and now hide part of the thatched roof and the green and white

stripes of the repainted summerhouse do not go right to the ground as they did in the earlier picture.

Two views taken from Archer House, the premises of Archer and Archer, solicitors for well over 200 years. The top picture is of Ely Fair in the market place in 1986 when it was held here, its traditional site, for the last time. To the left are the stalls of the Thursday Market which were temporarily moved at the time of the fair to the south side of the Market Place and along the High Street so that both market and fair could function on Thursdays. Then there was no Saturday market so the stalls only had to make way for the fair on one of the three days that it was held in spring and autumn.

A reception given for visiting French children in July 1949. More Ely people were there than French; in the back row, from left to right are Winifred Comins (with dark glasses), -?- , Daisy Coleridge, Gladys Houghton, Millie Morris, -?- , Miss Gladys Woolnough, Mrs Waters, -?- , and in the middle row; Essie Wilson, -?- , - ?- , Pamela Wilson, Betty Tedora, Colonel Goodwyn Archer, Mrs Bolton, -?- and Pamela Whitehead. On the left, at the front, are Jessie

Tebbitt and Dorothy Diver. No doubt these names and faces will conjure up memories for many local people.

Chapter 6

SCHOOLS, HOSPITALS AND PRISON

Girls at Broad Street School, *c.* 1946 (top) with, seated from left to right: Doreen Bowles, Norma Townsend, -?- , Audrey Ashman, Headmistress Miss Archer, Maisy Braybrook, Kathleen Drake, Daphne Baker and Margaret Watson. In the middle are -?-, Jean Lister, Janet -?- , -?- , -?- , Sheila Lemon, Shirley Martin, Shirley Page, Madelaine Racey, Gay Watkins, Margaret Lowe, Frances Moll (half hidden) and Janet Lane. Marjorie Cooper, Josephine Oakey, Vera Westley, Joan Prior, Jean Giddens, Daisy Travel, Shirley Ball, Molly Wigg, Marian Strawson, Ann Harding, Denise Wellington, Maureen Fitch, Rosemary Osborne, -?- , stand at the back. A group of boys and girls, perhaps surprisingly, more formerly dressed in the dark red and grey uniform of St Mary's Church of England School, pose in 1996; note that two of the girls wear trousers.

The National School in Silver Street (bottom). A typically mid-nineteenth-century school built by Teulon. In the centre is the headteacher's house which separated the boys from the girls. In 1933 this school took the name Ely Needham's Senior Boys' school (Needham's founded 1740). After various changes St Mary's Church of England Junior Mixed School was formed and housed in both Silver Street and Broad Street premises. In 1971 the school moved into new buildings at High Barns. The Silver Street buildings were demolished in 1972 and two houses were built on the site in around 1977;

part of the school wall has survived at the front. The fourteenth-century spire of St Mary's church, in St Mary's Street, is behind the Silver Street buildings.

Ely High School for Girls, 1917 (top). In 1913 it was advertised as 'A public Secondary Day School with a Preparatory Department for Girls and Boys under the Isle of Ely County Council'. Dorothy Defew, second from the left at the back, gained a London Honours Degree in English at the Royal Holloway College. She taught English, was deputy-headmistress, and acting headmistress for a year and then left Ely for a post at a teachers' training college but soon returned. She instilled a love of English poetry and literature into generations of girls until, after thirty years, she retired in 1964. A group of sixth form students at the City of Ely Community College, with some of the staff, provide a contrast with the formality of the earlier group.

The Theological College was founded in 1876 and housed in this building from 1881 until its closure in 1964. The building is now used by the King's School and is known as Hereward Hall. The cottage on the right was demolished long ago although some local people can remember a brewery employee who lived there and always wore a woolly hat, an overall under a tweed coat and black lace-up boots. The layout of the roads around Barton Square has been modernised but there is still a red telephone box in use.

It was built around 1880 on the site of a building that, for a short time during the seventeenth century, was part workhouse, part school and part bridewell. Ely Porta, the great gateway to the former monastery, housed the Prior's prison and the manor court from the end of the fourteenth century until the mid-sixteenth century. During the nineteenth century the Porta was used by the grammar school (the King's School) and now accommodates the school's senior library. The main changes to be seen are in the road signs, parking spaces and road layout with small roundabouts and traffic calming humps.

From the opposite side of Barton Square is another red brick building now known as Old Hereward.

The Jews Free School pictured when part of the school was evacuated to Ely in around 1939 (bottom). W. Martin Lane, well known as the photographer of the 1947 floods, ran a model-making club for the boys, almost certainly in Old Hereward though the room cannot be identified. The other adults are headmaster Dr Bernstein on the left and Bert Chinery who helped to run the club. At the back on the right is Maurice Solomons; no doubt others will be recognised by their wartime family hosts and hostesses. A group of King's School students in the same

building, a few years ago, intent on making objects of pewter during an after school activity time.

Outside the main entrance of the Royal Air Force Hospital, Ely all is ready for inspection by Diana, Princess of Wales when she visited Ely in 1987 (top); from then until it closed in 1992 it was The Princess of Wales RAF Hospital. It had been hurriedly built on land that was part of New Barns Farm in preparation for the Second World War. From the 1950s, Ely citizens were admitted as patients but subsequently most of the building was demolished and now, renamed the Princess of Wales Hospital, it deals with minor injuries and, increasingly, has clinics held by consultants from Addenbrooke's Hospital, Cambridge. New houses built during the last decade of the twentieth century almost fill the site; the tower of the hospital is seen on the right. From 1969-92 an Armstrong Whitworth NF (T) 14 'guarded' the entrance from Lynn Road.

This view was taken between the wars, probably *c.* 1930, from the cathedral west tower looking northwards toward Paradise before the Leisure Centre, Paradise Pool, and the Skate Park were built. This sports field is to the top left of the photo with Deacon's Lane and the partly completed New Barns estate in the distance. To the right the spire of the cemetery chapels with, nearer, early council houses in Brays Lane; the latter demolished to make way for a car park. High Street

Chapter 7

THE CHANGING SCENE

runs across the front with, from the left, the roofs of Cutlack's, Bonnett's and the Bell Hotel. The 1920s was a time of small changes and very gradual expansion in Ely.

From the cathedral west tower, *c*. 1986 the three gables of Bedford House, built in around 1800 by Thomas Page, dominate this view of St Mary's Street (top). It became, from 1824-1844, the headquarters of the Bedford Level Corporation, then a family home until 1905 when, for just over fifty years, it was the home of Ely High School for Girls. The main house is now part residential, part a day centre. The single storey building to the right was used by the river authority until 1968. The area where various huts were is now filled with a number of small flats, John Beckett Court, and, facing onto Chapel Street, Vera James House which provides twenty-four hour care. In the 2002 photograph a wider area is covered so part of the new developments around Ely can be seen in the distance.

St Mary's Street, *c.* 1908 (bottom). Before the Second World War, the tall Georgian houses on the right were the homes, from the left, of Dr Maurice Smith, the Townleys, Mrs Steele and the Evans; the latter well-known Ely solicitors. The white building was the White Lion pub until 1970, the corner house the home of the Punchards and then the Pratt family; it is now an alternative health centre. Beyond are the Thomas Parsons' Charity almshouses. Dr Smith's house remains but a new house was built where the others stood and then in 1991 St Mary's surgery opened here. Opposite was a

grocers for much of the last century, though a bookshop for a short time; now it is Snippets, a hairdressers.

left is the Wheatsheaf public house, an old barn and Waterloo House. Part of the house goes back to the fifteenth century. The barn, perhaps of the seventeenth century, was again thatched in 1995 with Norfolk reed from Cley on the east coast, by Tim Ellis; the woven reed on the underside was left intact. The pub has been replaced by a private house and the row of small cottages on the right by Fairfax Court, a sheltered housing complex. In the earlier photograph the chimney of the first of the two Red White and Blue public houses is probably that above the small 1930s car.

Taken between the wars, the top picture shows the cottages on the right, known as Waterloo Place. On the

In Chequer Lane, which links High Street and Market Street, is the former Salem chapel built in 1840 and used by the Independent Baptists until around 1875. It was later, about 1890, used by the Church of England Men's Society. During the 1940s and '50s it was used by A.E. Dean, plumbers, and towards the end of the last century as a store. Seen here before it was refurbished in 2001 when the interior was converted in a way suitable to house a dental practice. The recent photograph shows two members of the Chequer Hall practice outside in 2002, on the right of the doorway is the head of the practice with one of his assistants.

During the nineteenth century the Red White and Blue public house was right on the corner of Chiefs Street, once known as Tisse Lane, and West Fen Road. In 1965 it moved into a new building further back on the same site. Local people, seen outside the already closed pub (top) wanted it to re-open rather than be demolished, so they got up a petition. It was unsuccessful and in 2001 a group of houses and flats were built on the site now known as Bakers Corner. So named because archaeologists concluded that, possibly, there had been a Saxon bakery on the site.

eald Way, around 1998 is named after the once-nearby Beald Farm and Beald Drove, the latter a place for family Sunday walks in the 1930s. Photographs are rare of areas recently developed on the outskirts of Ely but this pair of images at least serves to show that change has been sudden and dramatic. The view of distant farmland totally obliterated by part of the housing estate that sprang up during 2000-2001. Still recognisable are the two trees on the right and Anglian Water's pumping station, which deals with sewage, hidden within the small fenced area.

These railway carriages (top), one a Pullman of 1860 and the other a first class passenger, came off the lines in 1923 and provided a home for George (Nibby) and Flo Lee on Lynn Road for fifty-seven years. They brought up their children, two girls and a boy here. The carriages, after a year-long search to find the right buyer, were sold in 1985 and taken near to Grimsby. They were to be restored and are perhaps back on the rails if suitable wheels have been found. Bungalows now occupy the site at the end of Buckingham Drive.

The Walbro sold wirelesses, and in the days when accumulators were used to provide power to them, the heavy acid-filled batteries could be recharged there. The Walbro, as this shop was known, the third building from the right, bottom picture, also sold cycles. It was run by the Wallis family and it was Ken Wallis who invented and flew the auto-gyro featured in James Bond films. Later carpets, then antiques and once again cycles were sold here until it became very dilapidated and was demolished. Within the last three years a house and office have been built here. On the right, behind the wall, during the 1920s was Barnard and Butcher

monumental and general masons; the business continued under the name of Barnard during the 1930s. On the left is part of Minster Place.

about half a century. J. & J. Wade, optometrists, opened here in1998 after moving from Market Street. To the south the smaller building in Minster Place, where goods mainly from Scotland are sold today, was where Mr Cass opened his garage and later Mr Pryor had a workshop. Between this and the corner, at one time, Mr Wolfendon, followed by Mr Jefferson Smith, had dental surgeries. The corner was rebuilt and by 1968 the area occupied by the workshop and round the back of the corner into High Street, which had included the offices of C. Hill & Son, was also rebuilt. For a while the Cathedral Grill and Restaurant was here, now a solicitor's office.

The Prudential Corner, c. 1908 (top). It was known as this locally because the company converted this building for its offices in 1920 and used them for

Many people will remember this shop, restaurant and bakery when it was run by Master Baker Vernon Cross, son of Frederick T. Cross who had acquired these premises in 1892. Vernon built up a idiosyncratic personal local museum in the restaurant; his interesting collection was dispersed – sold at auction – when he retired in 1964. Part of the building goes back to the sixteenth century and now the whole has been incorporated into the Royal Standard public house een decorated with hanging baskets in he summer of 2001. Lower down the hill, now the Lotus Inn, a chinese estaurant, was Miss Brewster's who advertised 'ladies' and children's outfitters; woollen knitted garments and wools'.

This slaughterhouse (top) at Willow Walk, near the river, pictured after it had closed in 1981, served local butcher A.S. Lemmon for many years and like many other small sites has recently had a house built on it. Close to the river too is Waterside, once the main way into the city when the river was an important route for people and trade. After the Second World War this area was relatively run down but then became a General Improvement Area. It is now a desirable place to live and perhaps to collect antiques at Waterside Antiques Centre and from antiques' fairs held in the nearby Ely Maltings.

Tesco opened here in Broad Street, almost opposite the present car park entrance in 1982; this was to be the second branch in Ely as there is another store on the Market Place. A large garden, once that of brewer Harlock's house facing the river and situated between Back Lane and Hythe Lane, was surrounded by a high wall. This garden was replaced by two small factory units in post war years, and when Tesco opened a larger store near the railway station this branch closed. Now a varied group of houses has been built between Broad Street and the river, named Cardinals Way. Although cardinals are not readily associated with modern Ely, five have been in the

distant past, for example Lewis of Luxembourg and John Morton, both fifteenth-century bishops of Ely.

Until the 1930s, when they were demolished to make a wider entrance to the wood yard, three jettied Tudor cottages stood here. The site was later occupied by a Jewson's (top) and now, in 2002, Jubilee Park has been created. Although officially opened in February 2002 it was promptly closed fo the next four months before being open to the public on 1 June. The Park stretches from Broad Street to the river with a wide path winding through grassed areas, flower beds and trees among which are alders, mountain ashes and birches. At present there are seats and a range of other amenities, including a bandstand, are planned for the future. In the distance are the two boathouses across the water, on Babylon.

Back Hill. In the earlier photograph the Royal Oak, now a private house, s on the left and on the right the Rifleman or Volunteer (closed soon after he First World War), which sold ale and tout from Legge's brewery in Newnham Street. The small grassed area which replaced the shop which had succeeded the Rifleman was planted ather hurriedly in 1987 with a couple of mall lime trees. This was in preparation or the Queen's second official visit, vith the Duke of Edinburgh, for the distribution of the Royal Maundy. In both photographs a larger house known s The Close, the home of Major

Roberson and his family (one of the daughters Mrs Beryl Buckwell is now in her nineties) is hidden behind the trees.

BACK HILL. ELY.

The entrance to Angel Drove, seen here (top) around 1983 shows the station goods yard buildings on the left. The drove was an old grassy tree lined, often muddy, way which led from Station Road to Cambridge Road and provided a pleasant walk in summer. The roadway is now a bypass and as it leaves Station Road there are business premises on either side and beyond Tesco's entrance, the Cambridgeshire Business Park on the south east side. This is a rapidly expanding area with over twenty high technology and quality production companies, little of which can be seen in the photograph which looks towards Ely. Privately run Lancaster Way Business Park on a former airfield site off Witchford Road is equally flourishing but with less high-tech businesses.

Station Road between the wars (bottom). Like Angel Drove, which turns off to the right, the road has changed almost unrecognisably within living memory. Once, a row of plane trees lined the west side beyond the entrance to the drove, partly hiding railway buildings and a goods yard; later a small furniture factory was there and in May 1994 Tesco opened. On the opposite side were three public houses – King Charles in the Oak, the Crown and the Railway Inn – coal merchant Hawkes' house and Coote and Warren's coal yard where today Standen's predominates. In the distance is Ely railway crossing and underpass; here is the railway bridge which holds the

doubtful distinction of being the second most 'knocked into' railway bridge in the country; unfortunately many drivers do not know the height of their vehicles!

The cathedral, seen above the old orchard (top) before the present Broad Street car park was created in 1965. In the 1930s the orchard, mainly of apple trees, was managed by Mr Boulter and later by Mr Newman. It ran alongside a private garden rented from the Dean and Chapter which is now the block of land at the back of the hairdresser's and other shops on Fore Hill. Part of the leather factory is on the right. Again the view is different, and although the second photo was taken from a lower viewpoint because of the growth of the large willow tree, it clearly shows the change from orchard to car park and the absence of the factory.